FOLLOW HIM

A 35-DAY CALL TO
LIVE FOR CHRIST
NO MATTER THE COST

DAVID PLATT

TYNDALE
MOMENTUM®

The nonfiction imprint of
Tyndale House Publishers

Visit Tyndale online at www.tyndale.com.

TYNDALE, Tyndale Momentum, and the Tyndale Momentum logo are registered trademarks of Tyndale House Publishers. Tyndale Momentum is the nonfiction imprint of Tyndale House Publishers, Carol Stream, Illinois.

Follow Him: A 35-Day Call to Live for Christ No Matter the Cost

The devotions in *Follow Him* are adapted from *Follow Me: A Call to Die. A Call to Live,* published in 2013 by Tyndale House Publishers under ISBN 978-1-4143-7328-7.

Designed by Mark Anthony Lane II

Published in association with Yates & Yates (www.yates2.com).

Unless otherwise indicated, all Scripture quotations are taken from ESV® Bible (The Holy Bible, English Standard Version) copyright © 2001 by Crossway, a publishing ministry of Good News Publishers. Used by permission. All rights reserved.

The Scripture quotation marked NIV is taken from the Holy Bible, *New International Version*®, *NIV*®. Copyright © 1973, 1978, 1984, 2011 by Biblica, Inc.® Used by permission. All rights reserved worldwide.

For information about special discounts for bulk purchases, please contact Tyndale House Publishers at csresponse@tyndale.com, or call 1-800-323-9400.

ISBN 978-1-4964-4069-3

Printed in China

26	25	24	23	22	21	20
7	6	5	4	3	2	1

The author's royalties from this book will go toward promoting the glory of Christ in all nations.

INTRODUCTION

ONE OF THE MOST influential things I have ever read is a little booklet called "Born to Reproduce" by Dawson Trotman, founder of The Navigators. In a matter of only a few pages, Trotman builds the case that "every person who is born into God's family is to multiply." Yet, he maintains, most Christians are not multiplying. He laments, "In every Christian audience, I am sure there are men and women who have been Christians for five, ten, or twenty years but who do not know of one person who is living for Jesus Christ today because of them."[1] This is a problem, Trotman says, and it's the reason the gospel has not yet spread to the nations.

By God's design, he has wired his children for spiritual reproduction. He has woven into the fabric of every single Christian's DNA a desire and ability to reproduce. God has formed, fashioned, and even filled Christians with his own Spirit for this very purpose.

To be a disciple of Jesus is to make disciples of Jesus. This has been true ever since the first century, when Jesus invited four men to follow him. His words echo throughout this book: "Follow me, and I will make you fishers of men."[2]

More important than searching for fish all over the Sea of Galilee, these men would spread the gospel all over the world. They would give their lives by not simply *being* disciples of Jesus, but by sacrificially *making* disciples of Jesus. And God's design for twenty-first-century disciples is exactly the same. Jesus calls every one of his disciples to make disciples who make disciples until the gospel penetrates every group of people in the world.

But somewhere along the way, we lost sight of what it means to be a disciple, and we have laid aside Jesus' command to *make* disciples. Tragically, we have minimized what it means to be a follower of Jesus, and we have virtually ignored the biblical expectation that we fish for men. The result has been a rampant "spectator mentality" that skews discipleship across the church, stifles the spread of the gospel around the world, and ultimately sears the heart of what it means for each of us to be a Christian.

Becoming a Christian involves responding to the gracious invitation of God in Christ. Being a Christian involves leaving behind superficial religion for supernatural regeneration. As we follow Christ, he transforms our minds, desires, wills, relationships, and ultimate reason for living. Every disciple of Jesus exists to make disciples of Jesus, here and among every people group on the planet. There are no spectators. We are all born to reproduce.

So, let me ask you: Do you desire to reproduce your faith? Do you long to see people come to know Jesus Christ through your life? If the answer to these questions is *yes*, then I invite you, over the next thirty-five days, to take a closer look at what it means to be a true disciple; to become a fisher of men; to give up your life, take up your cross, and *Follow Him*.

FOLLOW ME

Jesus spoke to them, saying, "I am the light of the world. Whoever follows me will not walk in darkness, but will have the light of life."

JOHN 8:12

FOUR FISHERMEN WERE STANDING by the sea one day when Jesus approached them. "Follow me," he said, "and I will make you fishers of men."[1] With that, Jesus beckoned these men to leave behind their professions, possessions, dreams, ambitions, family, friends, safety, and security. He bid them to abandon everything. "If anyone is going to follow me," Jesus said, "he must deny himself."[2] In a world where everything revolves around self—protect yourself, promote yourself, preserve yourself, entertain yourself, comfort yourself, take care of yourself—Jesus says, "Slay yourself."

And that's exactly what happened with these four fishermen. According to Scripture and tradition, they paid a steep price for following Jesus. Peter was crucified upside down, Andrew was crucified in Greece, James was beheaded, and John was exiled.

Yet they believed it was worth the cost. In Jesus, these men found someone worth losing everything for. In Christ, they encountered a love that surpassed comprehension, a satisfaction that superseded circumstances, and a purpose that transcended every other possible pursuit in this world. They eagerly, willingly, and gladly lost their lives to know, follow, and proclaim him. In the footsteps of Jesus, these first disciples discovered a path worth giving their lives to tread.

Two thousand years later, we seem to have wandered from the path. Somewhere along the way, amid varying cultural tides and popular church trends, we have minimized Jesus' summons to total abandonment. Scores of men, women, and children have been told that becoming a follower of Jesus simply involves acknowledging certain facts or saying certain words. But this is not true. Disciples like Peter, Andrew, James, and John show us that the call to follow Jesus is not simply an invitation to pray a prayer; it's a summons to lose our lives.

There is indescribable joy to be found, deep satisfaction to be felt, and an eternal purpose to be fulfilled in dying to ourselves and living for him.

Ask the Lord to give you the grace to follow him in faith and in glad obedience.

THE GATE
IS NARROW

What will it profit a man if he gains the whole world and forfeits his soul? Or what shall a man give in return for his soul?

MATTHEW 16:26

IS IT POSSIBLE to profess to be a Christian and yet not know Christ? Absolutely. In fact, according to Jesus, it's *probable*.

In the Sermon on the Mount, Jesus says to his disciples:

> Not everyone who says to me, "Lord, Lord," will enter the kingdom of heaven, but the one who does the will of my Father who is in heaven. On that day many will say to me, "Lord, Lord, did we not prophesy in your name, and cast out demons in your name, and do many mighty works in your name?" And then will I declare to them, "I never knew you; depart from me, you workers of lawlessness."
>
> MATTHEW 7:21-23

We're all prone to spiritual deception—every single one of us. Jesus isn't talking about ir-religious atheists, pagans, and heretics here. He's talking about good, religious people—men and women associated with him who assume their eternity is safe but who will be shocked one day to find out it's not. Though they pro-fessed belief in Jesus and even did all kinds of work in his name, they never truly knew him.

This is why Jesus' words are so critical for us to hear. When he says, "Enter by the narrow gate. For the gate is wide and the way is easy that leads to destruction, and those who enter by it are many. For the gate is narrow and the way is hard that leads to life, and those who find it are few,"[1] he is exposing our dangerous tendency to gravitate toward that which is easy and popular.

But this is not the way of Jesus. He beckons us down a hard road, and the word he uses for "hard" is associated in other parts of the Bible with pain, pressure, tribulation, and persecution. The way of Jesus is hard to follow, and it's hated by many. But those who do follow in his footsteps will discover that there is far more pleasure to be experienced *in* him, indescribably greater power to be realized *with* him, and a much higher purpose to be accomplished *for* him than anything else this world has to offer.

> Pray that God would help you see
> that the narrow road that leads
> to life is worth following because
> Christ himself is worth it.

10

GIVE UP EVERYTHING

He died for all, that those who live might no longer live for themselves but for him who for their sake died and was raised.

2 CORINTHIANS 5:15

IN *MY UTMOST FOR HIS HIGHEST*, Oswald Chambers writes,

> Suppose God tells you to do something that is an enormous test of your common sense, totally going against it. What will you do? Will you hold back? If you get into the habit of doing something physically, you will do it every time you are tested until you break the habit through sheer determination. And the same is true spiritually. Again and again you will come right up to what Jesus wants, but every time you will turn back at the true point of testing, until you are determined to abandon yourself to God in total surrender.[1]

Chambers's words challenge us to consider the seeming madness of Jesus' proclamation in the Gospel of Luke:

> If anyone comes to me and does not hate his own father and mother and wife and children and brothers and sisters, yes, and even his own life, he cannot be my disciple. Whoever does

not bear his own cross and come after
me cannot be my disciple. . . . Any one
of you who does not renounce all that
he has cannot be my disciple.[2]

To everyone else in the world, Jesus Christ's proclamation that we must hate our parents, siblings, spouse, children, and ourselves in order to follow him may seem mad, but to every Christian, these words are life.

Jesus Christ demands the same
unrestrained, adventurous spirit in
those who have placed their trust in
Him. . . . If a person is ever going to
do anything worthwhile, there will be
times when he must risk everything
by his leap in the dark. In the spiritual
realm, Jesus Christ demands that you
risk everything you hold on to or
believe through common sense, and
leap by faith into what He says.[3]

For the few who choose to abandon themselves to the will of God and put their trust in his character, following Jesus wherever he leads—no matter the cost—is the only thing that makes sense.

Confess your need for God's wisdom
and ask him to give you the grace
to entrust your entire life to him.

BELIEVE AND CONFESS

*With the heart one believes and is justified, and
with the mouth one confesses and is saved.*

ROMANS 10:10

IN JOHN'S GOSPEL, Jesus tells Nicodemus, "God so loved the world, that he gave his only Son, that whoever believes in him should not perish but have eternal life."[1] In the book of Acts, Paul and Silas tell the Philippian jailer, "Believe in the Lord Jesus, and you will be saved."[2] And according to the book of Romans, "If you confess with your mouth that Jesus is Lord and believe in your heart that God raised him from the dead, you will be saved."[3]

Based on these passages, you might conclude that believing in Jesus is all that's involved in becoming or being a Christian. This is absolutely true, but we must consider context to understand what the Bible means by *belief*. When Jesus called Nicodemus to believe in him, he was calling him to be born again—to begin an entirely new life devoted to following him.

Likewise, when the Philippian jailer believed in Christ, he knew he was joining a community of Christians who were being beaten, flogged, and imprisoned for their faith. The cost of following Christ was clear. In the same way, Paul told the Roman Christians that to believe in the saving resurrection of Jesus from the dead was to confess Jesus' sovereign lordship over their lives.

In each of these verses (and scores of others like them), belief in Jesus for salvation involves far more than mere intellectual assent. After all, even the demons *believe* that Jesus is the crucified and resurrected Son of God.[4] Such "belief" clearly doesn't save anyone. We all can publicly profess beliefs we don't hold, but only those who are obedient to the words of Christ will enter his Kingdom. If our lives do not reflect the fruit of following Jesus, then we are foolish to think we are his followers.

> Thank God that his salvation is all a work of grace. Ask him to continue to produce spiritual fruit in you by his Spirit.

REPENT AND CHANGE

The Lord is not slow to fulfill his promise as some count slowness, but is patient toward you, not wishing that any should perish, but that all should reach repentance.

2 PETER 3:9

I FIND IT INTERESTING that *repent* is the very first word out of Jesus' mouth in his ministry in the New Testament.[1] Repentance is a rich biblical term that signifies an elemental transformation in someone's mind, heart, and life. When people repent, they turn from walking in one direction to running in the opposite direction. From that point forward, they think differently, believe differently, feel differently, love differently, and live differently.

When Jesus said, "Repent," he was speaking to people who were rebelling against God in their sin and relying on themselves for their salvation. Jesus' predominantly Jewish audience believed that their family heritage, social status, knowledge of specific rules, and obedience to certain regulations were sufficient to make them right before God.

Jesus' call to repentance, then, was a summons for these people to renounce sin and all dependence on self for salvation. Only by turning from their sin—away from themselves and toward Jesus—could they be saved. Fundamentally, then, repentance involves renouncing a former way of life in favor of a new way of life.

This doesn't mean that when we become Christians, we suddenly become perfect. It means that we make a decided break with an old way of living and take a decisive turn to a new way of life as followers of our Lord Jesus. We literally die to our sin and to ourselves—our self-centeredness, self-consumption, self-righteousness, self-indulgence, self-effort, and self-exaltation. In the words of the apostle Paul, we can say, "I have been crucified with Christ. It is no longer I who live, but Christ who lives in me."[2]

As Christ begins to live in us, everything about us begins to change. Our minds change. Our desires change. Our wills change. Our relationships change. Ultimately, our reason for living changes. Possessions and position are no longer our priorities. Comfort and security are no longer our concerns. Safety is no longer our goal, because self is no longer our god. We now want God's glory more than we want our own lives.

The more we glorify God, the more we enjoy him and realize that this is what it means biblically to be a Christian.

Ask God to give you an increasing hatred of sin and an increasing reliance on him as you seek to walk in obedience.

PURSUED BY CHRIST

This is love, not that we have loved God but that he loved us and sent his Son to be the propitiation for our sins.

1 JOHN 4:10

FOR FAR TOO LONG, we have convinced one another that we are basically good people who have simply made some bad decisions. Whether we've lied or cheated or stolen or taken God's name in vain, we've all made mistakes. We just need to invite Jesus to come into our hearts, and he will forgive us of all these things.

But the reality of the gospel is that we do not become God's children as a result of our own initiative. Nor does he provide salvation primarily because of an invitation from us.

The truth is, before we were ever born, God was working to adopt us. While we were lying alone in the depths of our sin, God was planning to save us. And the only way we can become a part of the family of God is through a love entirely beyond our imagination and completely out of our control.

This is at the core of Christianity, yet we are prone to miss it when we describe becoming a follower of Jesus as "inviting him into our heart." Christianity does not begin with our pursuit of Jesus, but with his pursuit of us. Likewise, Christianity doesn't begin with an invitation we offer to Jesus, but with an invitation *he* offers to us. We have done nothing to warrant this invitation. Not only has Jesus initiated a relationship with us, he also allows us to be recipients of his grace.

When we realize that Jesus is the one who invites us to follow him, everything changes. Our souls are struck by the greatness of the one who has called us. We are overwhelmed by the magnitude of the words *follow me* because we are awed by the majesty of the "me" who says them. He is worthy of more than church attendance and casual association. He is worthy of total abandonment and supreme adoration.

Everyone who has ever been saved from their sins knows that they have been pursued by Jesus—and their lives haven't been the same since.

> Thank God for his mercy in saving you by sending Christ to die for your sins.

LOOK AT
THE CROSS

*If we say we have no sin, we deceive ourselves,
and the truth is not in us. If we confess our
sins, he is faithful and just to forgive us our sins
and to cleanse us from all unrighteousness.*

1 JOHN 1:8-9

IS IT TRUE that God hates the sin but loves the sinner? Well, yes, in one sense, but not completely. Fourteen times in the first fifty psalms alone, we read of God's hatred toward the sinner, his wrath toward the liar, and so on. And the Old Testament doesn't stand alone on this. In John 3—the same chapter where we find John 3:16, one of the most famous verses about God's love—we find one of the most neglected verses about God's wrath: "Whoever rejects the Son will not see life, for God's wrath remains on them."[1]

Sin is not something that exists outside of us. Sin is ingrained into the core of our being. We don't just sin; we exist as sinners. So, when Jesus went to the cross to die, he was not just taking the payment of sin, as if it were separate from us. Instead, he was paying the price that was due us as sinners. He was dying for us, in our place, as our substitute. In the words of Isaiah 53, "He was pierced for *our* transgressions; he was crushed for *our* iniquities; . . . and the LORD has laid on him the iniquity of *us* all."[2] When Jesus was pulverized under the weight of God's wrath on the cross, he experienced what you and I *deserve* to experience. He endured the full punishment that was due you and me as sinners.

Therefore, we must be careful not to lean

on comfortable clichés that rob the Cross of its meaning. At the Cross, God showed the full expression of both his wrath and his love, as Jesus was stricken, smitten, afflicted, wounded, crushed, and chastised for the sake of sinners.

Does God hate sinners? Absolutely. Look at the Cross. Jesus endured what we were due.

Does God love sinners? Absolutely. Look at the Cross. Jesus saved us from all we were due.

God is holy, possessing righteous wrath toward sin and sinners alike. Yet God is also merciful, possessing holy love toward sinners. And because of his grace, his mercy, and his love, *we* have been invited to follow him.

> Praise God for his holiness and his love displayed in the Cross of Christ.

ONE LOST SHEEP

The Son of Man came to seek and to save the lost.

LUKE 19:10

THE APOSTLE PAUL, in his letter to the Ephesians, writes,

> The God and Father of our Lord Jesus
> Christ . . . chose us in him before the
> foundation of the world, that we should
> be holy and blameless before him. In
> love he predestined us for adoption
> to himself as sons through Jesus
> Christ, according to the purpose of his
> will, to the praise of his glorious grace,
> with which he has blessed us in the
> Beloved.[1]

These words evoke awe and amazement, don't they? To consider that before the sun was ever formed, before a star was ever placed in the sky, before mountains were ever laid upon the earth, and before oceans were ever poured over the land, God Almighty on high set his sights on the Christian's soul. And not only did he plan to *love* his children, but he also *pursues* us with his love. Even though we have wandered away from him, he comes searching after us. Over and above our sinful rebellion and selfish resistance, God in Christ pursues his people.

Jesus describes this relentless pursuit in the parable of the lost sheep:

What man of you, having a hundred sheep, if he has lost one of them, does not leave the ninety-nine in the open country, and go after the one that is lost, until he finds it? And when he has found it, he lays it on his shoulders, rejoicing. And when he comes home, he calls together his friends and his neighbors, saying to them, "Rejoice with me, for I have found my sheep that was lost." Just so, I tell you, there will be more joy in heaven over one sinner who repents than over ninety-nine righteous persons who need no repentance.[2]

What an amazing picture of God's love for us. And then, in an act that must seem crazy to most people, God sent his Son to die on the cross for our sin so that we could be saved by him. Do you realize the wonder of this?

Thank God for pursuing you in your sin. Ask him to renew your joy as you consider his grace in the gospel.

THE MYSTERY OF MERCY

Blessed be the God and Father of our Lord Jesus Christ! According to his great mercy, he has caused us to be born again to a living hope through the resurrection of Jesus Christ from the dead.

1 PETER 1:3

GOD IS NOT the only one working in salvation. We must *choose* to receive or reject the mercy of God in Christ. The mystery of God's mercy in no way negates the nature of our responsibility. But lest we ever think that such a decision begins with an invitation borne out of our own initiative, the Bible clearly reminds us that, left to ourselves, we would be lost forever. The only reason we can seek Christ in our sinfulness is because Christ has sought us as our Savior.

The glory of the gospel is that the God of the universe reaches beyond the hardness of our hearts, overcoming our selfish resistance and sinful rebellion, and he saves us from ourselves. Such mercy magnifies God's pursuit of us and crucifies our pride before him. Praise God that he has not left the invitation to salvation up to sinful men and women who in their rebellion would never choose him. Praise God that he has taken the initiative to call and enable us to follow Jesus, so that in his overcoming grace we might find eternal satisfaction for our souls.

To be a Christian is to be loved by God, pursued by God, and found by God. To be a Christian is to realize that in your sin, you were separated from God's presence, and you deserved nothing but God's wrath. Yet despite your darkness and in your deadness, his light shone on you and his voice spoke to you, inviting you to follow him. His majesty captivated your soul and his mercy covered your sin, and by his death he brought you life. You are his child, not ultimately because of any good you have done—any prayers you have prayed, steps you have taken, or boxes you have checked—but solely because of the grace he has given.

> Confess to God that your salvation is based on his grace in Christ and not on your own wisdom or abilities.

COME TO ME

Come to me, all who labor and are heavy laden,
and I will give you rest. Take my yoke upon you,
and learn from me, for I am gentle and lowly in
heart, and you will find rest for your souls.

MATTHEW 11:28-29

CHRISTIANITY IS RADICALLY different from every other religion in the world. In every religion, a teacher (or series of teachers) prescribes certain paths to follow to honor God (or different gods) and experience salvation (however that is described).

Hindus believe that the path to remission of sins and liberation from the cycle of life and death is paved through homage to the goddess Ganga, represented by the Ganges River. In Islam, Muhammad pointed in the Koran to five pillars for Muslims to practice. In Buddhism, the Buddha's eightfold path is just one of four noble truths that he taught, alongside hundreds of other rules for Buddhists to follow. In Sikhism, ten gurus have pointed to one body of teaching as the way to truth and life.

But this is where Christianity stands alone. When Jesus came on the scene in human history and began calling followers to himself, he did not say, "Follow certain rules. Observe specific regulations. Perform ritual duties. Pursue a particular path." Instead, he said, "Follow *me.*"[1] With these two simple words, Jesus made clear that his primary purpose was not to instruct his disciples in a prescribed religion; his primary purpose was to invite his disciples into a personal relationship with him. He was not saying,

"Go this way to find truth and life." Instead, he was saying, "*I am* the way, and the truth, and the life."[2] The call of Jesus was, "Come to *me*. Find rest for your souls in *me*. Find joy in your heart from *me*. Find meaning in your life through *me*."

This extremely shocking and utterly revolutionary call is the essence of what it means to be a disciple of Jesus: We are not called to simply believe certain points or observe certain practices, but ultimately to cling to the person of Jesus as life itself.

No matter how many times we wash our bodies in a river or pray according to procedure; regardless of how many steps we take down a path or how many needy people we help; and despite our most passionate attempts to pray the right prayers, repeat the right words, sing the right songs, give the right gifts, and live the right lives, we cannot cover up the evil that is so deeply entrenched within our hearts. Our greatest need is not to do more or try harder. Our greatest need is a new heart.

Pray that God would give you confidence and assurance as you rest in the finished work of Jesus Christ.

NEVER ENOUGH

*When the goodness and loving kindness of God
our Savior appeared, he saved us, not because of
works done by us in righteousness, but according
to his own mercy, by the washing of regeneration
and renewal of the Holy Spirit, whom he poured
out on us richly through Jesus Christ our Savior.*

TITUS 3:4-6

DO YOU EVER feel as if your Christianity consists of nothing more than a list of truths to believe, things to do, and boxes to check to earn God's approval? In your efforts to pray, read the Bible, give, and serve in the church, do you ever feel that you can never do enough?

Nicodemus, a leader among the Jewish people in the first century, was like many professing Christians today, possessing a measure of belief in and respect for Jesus while ordering his life around the commands of Scripture. He prayed and went to worship. He read and even taught the Bible. He lived a good, decent, moral life, and he was an example to others. Everything was right on the outside, but something was wrong on the inside. Despite all the religious things he did, Nicodemus had no spiritual life in him. This is the curse of superficial religion.

Superficial religion involves a counterfeit Christian life that consists of nothing more than truths to believe and things to do, and it misses the essence of what it means to follow Jesus. Supernatural regeneration, on the other hand, involves an authentic Christian life that has been awakened by the Spirit, truth, love, passion, power, and purpose of Jesus.

So how did Jesus respond to the superficial

religion of Nicodemus? He told him, "Unless one is born of water and the Spirit, he cannot enter the kingdom of God."[1]

What does that mean?

Jesus refers here to a promise that God made to his people through the prophet Ezekiel:

I will sprinkle clean water on you, and you shall be clean from all your uncleannesses, and from all your idols I will cleanse you. And I will give you a new heart, and a new spirit I will put within you. And I will remove the heart of stone from your flesh and give you a heart of flesh. And I will put my Spirit within you, and cause you to walk in my statutes and be careful to obey my rules.[2]

Such cleansing is a gift from God, not based at all on your own merit, but altogether on God's mercy. That's why the Bible teaches that faith alone in Christ alone is the only way to salvation from sin. Faith is the *anti-work*. It's the realization that there is nothing you can do but trust in what has been done for you in the life, death, and resurrection of Jesus. Faith is the realization that God's pleasure in you will never be based on your performance for him. Instead, God's pleasure in you will always be based on Christ's performance for you.

> Ask God to reveal the areas in your life where your thoughts, words, and actions are not motivated by a genuine love for him. Pray that God would continually change you by his Spirit.

THE REVOLUTIONARY TRUTH OF THE GOSPEL

I will be merciful toward their iniquities,
and I will remember their sins no more.

HEBREWS 8:12

THE CLEAR MESSAGE of the Bible is that there is nothing we can do to make our hearts clean before a holy God. We can work constantly, pray fervently, give extravagantly, and love sacrificially, but our hearts will still be stained by sin.

I heard a story once about an Englishman who bought a Rolls-Royce. It had been advertised as the car that would never, ever, ever break down. So the man bought the Rolls-Royce at a hefty price and was driving it one day when, to his surprise, it broke down. He was far away from town, so he called Rolls-Royce and said, "Hey, you know this car that will never break down? Well, it's broken down." Immediately, a Rolls-Royce mechanic was sent via helicopter to the location where the car was broken down. The car was fixed, and the man went on his way. Naturally, the man expected to get a bill from Rolls-Royce. It was clearly expensive for them to provide such service (not often does a mechanic fly to where your car is broken down!), and he wanted to get the whole ordeal behind him. So when the bill had not yet come a few weeks later, the man called Rolls-Royce and said, "I'd like to go ahead and pay the bill for my auto repairs so that we can get this behind us." Rolls-Royce responded, "Sir, we are deeply sorry, but we have absolutely no record of anything ever having gone wrong with your car."

Consider the wonder. For all who come to Christ and receive a new heart from him, the God of the universe looks at you and says, "I have absolutely no record of anything ever having gone wrong in your life." The invitation is clear: Come to Christ and he will cleanse your heart. This is the revolutionary truth of the gospel: We do not have to work to wash away our sins. As we turn from our sin to trust in Christ, we receive a new, clean heart, and God in his grace remembers our sins no more.

> Thank God that he does not treat you as your sins deserve, and rejoice in the good news of the gospel.

THE GOOD NEWS OF CHRIST

*Bless the LORD, O my soul, and all that is within me,
bless his holy name! Bless the LORD, O my soul, and forget
not all his benefits, who forgives all your iniquity,
who heals all your diseases, who redeems your life from
the pit, who crowns you with steadfast love and mercy.*

PSALM 103:1-4

ALL AROUND THE WORLD TODAY, people are equating the gospel of Jesus Christ with physical healing and material prosperity. "Come to Jesus," they say, "and you will receive physical reward." But that is not the essence of the gospel. Yes, Jesus is able to heal physical maladies; and yes, Jesus has authority over painful diseases, but this is not the central message of Christ. We don't go throughout America, saying, "Trust in Christ, and cancer will be gone." We don't go throughout Africa, declaring, "Trust in Christ, and HIV/AIDS will be no more." We don't go anywhere crying, "Trust in Christ, and health and wealth will come your way."

That is not the Good News of Christ, for the Good News of Christ is so much greater than that. The Good News of Christ is not primarily that Jesus will heal you of all your sicknesses right now, but ultimately that Jesus will forgive you of all your sins forever. The Good News of Christ is not that if you muster enough faith in Jesus, you can have physical and material reward on this earth. The Good News of Christ is that when you have childlike faith in Jesus, you will be reconciled to God for eternity.

We mustn't be like the paralyzed man and his friends in Matthew 9, approaching Jesus as a miracle worker who was merely able to meet immediate physical needs. To their surprise, though they expected Jesus to heal the man physically, Jesus' first response was "Take heart, my son; your sins are forgiven."[1]

In these words, he made it clear that the ultimate priority of his coming was not simply to relieve suffering, but to sever the cause of suffering—*sin*—at the root.

Pray that God would give you a heart to pursue him, the Giver, and not merely his gifts. Ask him to help you live for eternal treasure rather than short-lived pleasures.

DAY 14

THE ESSENCE OF THE CHRISTIAN LIFE

You have died, and your life is hidden with Christ in God.

COLOSSIANS 3:3

SO OFTEN WE ASSUME that the essence of the Christian life is being forgiven of our sin. Many professing Christians are stuck here, believing that Jesus has cleansed them from their sins, yet they are lacking true, authentic, real, radical change in their lives.

This is not the way it's supposed to be. As God promises in Ezekiel, "I will give you a new heart, and a new spirit I will put within you. . . . I will put my Spirit within you, and cause you to walk in my statutes and be careful to obey my rules."[1] The meaning behind these words is mind-blowing. When you come to Jesus, he not only forgives you of your sin, but he also fills you with his Spirit. Feel the magnitude of this: When you come to Jesus, he puts the source of his life in the center of your life.

This is the heart of Jesus' call to follow him. When you become a Christian, you die and Jesus becomes your life. To paraphrase Paul, "You have died with Christ, and you're not even alive anymore. Instead, Christ is alive in you, and the only way you live is by faith in him."[2]

Paul later writes, "If Christ is in you, although the body is dead because of sin, the Spirit is life because of righteousness. If the Spirit of him who raised Jesus from the dead dwells in you, he who raised Christ Jesus from the dead will also give life to your mortal bodies through his Spirit who dwells in you."[3]

This is the stunning message of Christianity: Jesus died for you so that he might live in you. Jesus doesn't merely improve your old nature; he imparts to you an entirely new nature—one that is completely united with his.

When you come to Jesus, his Spirit fills your spirit. His love becomes your love. His joy becomes your joy. His mind becomes your mind. His desires become your desires. His will becomes your will. His purpose becomes your purpose. His power becomes your power. The Christian life thus becomes nothing less than the outliving of the indwelling Christ.

> Thank God for the gift of his
> Spirit. Praise the Spirit for
> giving you new life in Christ.

FISHERS OF MEN

*Whoever does not bear his own cross and
come after me cannot be my disciple.*

LUKE 14:27

JESUS SAID, "FOLLOW ME, and I will make you fishers of men."[1] Using imagery drawn from their long-standing vocation, Jesus summoned his disciples to an all-consuming mission. More important than searching for fish all over the sea, they would spread the gospel all over the world. As a result of *being* disciples of Jesus, they would *make* disciples of Jesus.

The book of Matthew ends with Jesus on a mountainside, saying to these same disciples, "Go therefore and make disciples of all nations, baptizing them in the name of the Father and of the Son and of the Holy Spirit, teaching them to observe all that I have commanded you. And behold, I am with you always, to the end of the age."[2]

Somewhere between Matthew 4 and Matthew 28, Jesus transformed these disciples into disciple *makers*, and by the time they got to that mountain in Matthew 28, they were eager to tell everyone about the life, death, and resurrection of Jesus. Having been forgiven of their sin and soon to be filled with God's Spirit, they would give their lives not simply to *being* disciples of Jesus, but to sacrificially *making* disciples of Jesus. Fishing for men would become central for them—and costly to them.

Tradition tells us that Peter preached the

gospel to thousands at Pentecost and eventually was crucified upside down. Similar traditions tell us that Andrew was crucified while preaching the gospel in Greece; Judas (not Iscariot) was clubbed to death for ministering near modern-day Turkey; Thomas was speared through his side while making disciples in India; James was beheaded; Philip was stoned; and Matthew was burned at the stake, all for preaching the gospel. As a result of being disciples of Jesus, every one of these men literally gave their lives to making disciples of Jesus.

As Jesus transformed their minds, they became convicted that others needed to hear the gospel. As Jesus transformed their desires, they longed for people to hear the gospel. As Jesus transformed their wills, they were compelled to give their lives proclaiming the gospel. As Jesus transformed their relationships, they loved people enough to share the gospel with them, even though it cost them everything they had. As Jesus transformed their very purpose for living, every disciple was sacrificially committed to making disciples—and the trajectory of their lives was never the same.

Ask God to give you faith and
obedience as you seek to obey
Christ's great commission. Pray
that God would replace the fear
of man with a right fear of him.

SUPERNATURALLY COMPELLED

What you have heard from me in the presence of many witnesses entrust to faithful men, who will be able to teach others also.

2 TIMOTHY 2:2

IF CHRISTIANITY MERELY consists of a list of dutiful dos and don'ts on top of principles to believe and practices to observe, then we don't have much to share with the world. Further, if being a Christian is merely a matter of superficial religion, then no amount of persuasion will convince us that we need to step out of our comfort zones, alter our priorities, sacrifice our possessions, risk our reputations, and potentially even lose our lives to share Christ with others.

However, if Christianity involves supernatural regeneration whereby the God of the universe reaches down his hand of mercy into the depths of our souls, forgives us of all our sin, and fills us with his Spirit, then a spectator mentality is spiritually inconceivable. For people whose hearts, minds, wills, and relationships have been radically turned upside down by the person of Christ, the purpose of Christ will reign supreme.

If you are truly a disciple of Jesus, you will be supernaturally compelled to make disciples of Jesus. True followers of Jesus do not need to be convinced, cajoled, persuaded, or manipulated into making disciples of all nations. Everyone who follows Jesus biblically will fish for men globally.

The fruit of following Jesus is a new heart with a new mind, new desires, a new will, a new way of relating to people around you, and a new purpose. "Follow me," Jesus said, "and I will make you fishers of men."[1] This is not a solicitation to tread a path of superficial religion. This is an invitation to taste a pleasure that can be found only in a supernatural relationship with Jesus. He beckons you to allow your heart to be captivated by his greatness and your life to be changed by his grace. Turn from your *sin* and your *self* and trust in Jesus as the all-sovereign, all-satisfying Savior of your soul.

Ask God to empower you by his Spirit as you seek to follow Christ faithfully in accordance with his Word.

LORD AND SAVIOR

*What we proclaim is not ourselves, but Jesus Christ as
Lord, with ourselves as your servants for Jesus' sake.*

2 CORINTHIANS 4:5

WHEN FOLLOWERS OF CHRIST share stories of how they became Christians, they often say something along the lines of, "I decided to make Jesus my personal Lord and Savior." Initially and ultimately, of course, it's wonderful to hear brothers and sisters recount the moment when their hearts were opened to the incomprehensibly passionate love of God—a love that now captivates them in an intimately personal relationship with Jesus.

But this statement also minimizes the inherent authority of Jesus. Surely no one can *decide* to make him Lord. Jesus is Lord regardless of what you or I decide. The Bible is clear that one day "every knee should bow, in heaven and on earth and under the earth, and every tongue confess that Jesus Christ is Lord."[1] The question is not whether we will make Jesus Lord. The real question is whether you or I will *submit* to his lordship. This is the essence of conversion.

On an even deeper level, all too often our "decision" to "make Jesus our personal Lord and Savior" fosters a customized Christianity that revolves around a personal Christ that we create for ourselves. Slowly, subtly, we take the Jesus of the Bible and twist him into someone with whom we are a little more comfortable. We dilute what he says about the cost of following him, we disregard what he says about those who choose not to follow him, we ignore what he says about materialism, and we functionally miss what he says about mission. We pick and choose what we like and don't like from Jesus' teachings. In the end, we create a nice, inoffensive, politically correct, middle-class, American Jesus who looks just like us and thinks just like us.

But Jesus is not customizable. He has not left himself open to interpretation, adaptation, innovation, or alteration. He has spoken clearly through his Word, and we have no right to "personalize him." Instead, he revolutionizes *us*. He transforms our minds through his truth. As we follow Jesus, we believe Jesus, even when his Word confronts (and often contradicts) the deeply held assumptions, beliefs, and convictions of our lives, our families, our friends, our cultures, and sometimes even our churches. As we take Jesus at his word, we proclaim Jesus to the world, for we realize that he is not merely a personal Lord and Savior who is worthy of our individual approval. Ultimately, Jesus is the cosmic Lord and Savior who is worthy of everyone's eternal praise.

Acknowledge Christ's lordship over your life and over all things. Confess his authority and greatness.

THE SPIRIT OF TRUTH

Faith comes from hearing, and hearing through the word of Christ.

ROMANS 10:17

ACCORDING TO RESEARCH, many "Christians" no longer believe that God is the supreme Creator and Ruler of the universe. Such "Christians" believe that everyone is god or that maybe god is simply the realization of one's human potential. More than half of "Christians" don't believe that the Holy Spirit or Satan are real, and tens of millions don't believe that Jesus is the divine Son of God. Finally, almost half of "Christians" don't believe the Bible is completely true.[1]

Such "Christians" are not really Christians. It is impossible to follow Jesus yet disregard, discredit, and disbelieve his Word. Simply put, to follow Jesus is to believe Jesus.

Believing Jesus has been fundamental to following Jesus from the beginning. When you read through the Gospels and observe Jesus' interactions with his disciples, you see him continually teaching them truth and challenging their thinking. In every story and every conversation, Jesus turns his disciples' minds upside down with his words. Though he never enrolled his disciples in a formal school or sat them down in a classroom, Jesus used every situation, every conversation, every miracle, and every moment to mold their minds to become like his.

Then, as Jesus prepared his disciples for his death and departure, he promised them his

Spirit, "the Spirit of truth . . . [who] will teach you all things and bring to your remembrance all that I have said to you."[2] (Note: According to Jesus, the Holy Spirit is real.) To be a disciple of Jesus was (and is) to be devoted to the words of Jesus. "If you abide in my word," Jesus says, "you are truly my disciples, and you will know the truth, and the truth will set you free. . . . If you abide in me, and my words abide in you, ask whatever you wish, and it will be done for you."[3]

From the start, the promises and privileges of following Jesus with your life were tied to believing Jesus with your mind. And according to Scripture, the minds, hearts, and lives of Christians revolve entirely around the words of Christ.

Pray that God would overcome any unbelief in you and give you faith to gladly submit to his Word.

THE REALITY OF THE RESURRECTION

Yet a little while and the world will see me no more,
but you will see me. Because I live, you also will live.

JOHN 14:19

ARE WE REALLY supposed to take literally everything Jesus said? Yes—because the authority of Jesus' words is tied to the reality of his resurrection. Think about it. If Jesus wasn't resurrected, then all of Christianity is a hoax and Christians are the most pitiably stupid people on the planet.[1]

But if Jesus *did* rise from the dead; if he did what no one else in all of history has ever done or will ever do—conquer death—then merely *accepting* what Jesus said isn't enough. We must orient *everything* in our lives around what he said.

Now, some people don't even believe that Jesus died on a cross, much less rose from the grave three days later. Many Muslims, for example, suggest that it was merely a man who *looked* like Jesus who was crucified that day. Others believe that though Jesus was crucified, he didn't actually die on the cross; he merely fainted and was unconscious, so people mistakenly thought he was dead. Others maintain that the tomb wasn't empty. Some people believe that when the women went to the tomb that first Easter morning, in their grief and shock over Jesus' death they went to the wrong tomb and mistakenly thought he had risen. Some claim that the disciples stole the body of Jesus.

Others allege that the disciples were merely delusional—or hallucinating—when they claimed they had seen Jesus alive after he died.

Nevertheless, hundreds of people claimed to have seen Jesus, some of whom ate, drank, and talked with him. Hallucinations don't normally eat and drink. Besides, in first-century Palestine, it was not in the disciples' best interests to proclaim the resurrection of Jesus, knowing that they could (and would) die for it.

Why belabor this point? Because if Jesus indeed rose from the dead, then we absolutely must listen to everything he says. The reality of his resurrection validates both the truthfulness and timelessness of his teaching. A resurrected Jesus is not just another religious teacher whose thoughts and opinions we can take or leave according to our preferences. Regardless of what we might say (or decide), *Jesus is Lord*. Consequently, regardless of what Jesus might say, we have no other option but to trust his word.

> Praise the risen Christ for his power over sin and death. Thank him for the promise of resurrection to all who trust in him.

HEAVEN AND HELL

*The wages of sin is death, but the free gift of
God is eternal life in Christ Jesus our Lord.*

ROMANS 6:23

PERHAPS ONE OF THE most culturally contro-
versial issues Jesus spoke about was hell. Hell,
according to Jesus, is a place of conscious tor-
ment and utter darkness.[1] Elsewhere in the New
Testament, hell is described as a place of never-
ending destruction where people are separated
from the presence of the Lord and the power of
his might.[2]

Thankfully, Jesus spoke just as clearly about
heaven. He proclaimed about himself, "I am the
resurrection and the life. Whoever believes in
me, though he die, yet shall he live, and everyone
who lives and believes in me shall never die."[3]
Indeed, Jesus said, "Whoever believes in [me]
should not perish but have eternal life."[4] We find
comfort in the passages where Jesus promises his
disciples that he is preparing a place for them,[5]
a place where one day all who believe in him
will dwell with God in "a new heaven and a new
earth," where God "will wipe away every tear
from their eyes, and death shall be no more, nei-
ther shall there be mourning, nor crying, nor
pain anymore, for the former things have passed
away."[6] Over and over again, Jesus promised
everlasting joy and eternal life to all who turn
from themselves and their sin to trust in him.

True belief in both heaven and hell radically changes the way we live on earth. We are

encouraged by the hope of heaven, and we are compelled by the horror of hell. We know that this world is not all that exists. We know that every person on the planet is here for only a brief moment, and an eternity lies ahead of us all— an eternity filled with either ever-increasing delight or never-ending damnation.

So Jesus' words make sense: "Follow me, and I will make you fishers of men."[7] If you and I know and believe that Jesus came to save us—*from* hell and *for* heaven—then we have no choice but to spend our lives on earth making that salvation known. If the people sitting next to us at a coffee shop, studying next to us in the library, working next to us in the office, or living next to us in our neighborhoods may be on a road that leads to everlasting suffering, then we *must* tell them about the Savior who leads to eternal life and everlasting satisfaction. Anything less makes no sense, according to what we believe.

> Pray that God would fill you with hope as you anticipate being with Christ in heaven. Ask him to give you an urgency to share the gospel in light of the reality of hell.

SPIRITUAL BATTLE

*In him all the fullness of God was pleased
to dwell, and through him to reconcile to
himself all things, whether on earth or in
heaven, making peace by the blood of his cross.*

COLOSSIANS 1:19–20

CHRISTIANS SOMETIMES SAY, "When Jesus died on the cross, he died just for me." Without question, there is truth here, for Jesus personally died for you and me.[1] But we must not stop there. According to Jesus' own words, he died so that "repentance for the forgiveness of sins should be proclaimed in his name to all nations."[2]

We live in a fallen world of sin, suffering, and death. For centuries, creation longed for a coming king who would conquer all these things. That king came in the person of Jesus Christ. He did what no one else in history has ever done or will ever do again, and now he is "seated . . . at [God's] right hand in the heavenly places, far above all rule and authority and power and dominion, and above every name that is named, not only in this age but also in the one to come."[3]

He is not seated there simply to watch what is happening on earth. Through his Spirit, whom he sent, he is leading his people to proclaim his truth in every corner of the earth.

As followers of Christ, every one of us finds ourselves on the front lines of a spiritual battle that is raging for the souls of men and women right around us and all around the world. The all-sovereign Son of God, our Savior, is above us, sitting in the seat of heavenly command, with all authority in heaven and on earth. Day and night, he intercedes for us, and for the benefit of every person on the planet who remains captive to sin, Satan, and death, he is committed to giving us everything we need to tell them, "There is Good News. Turn from sin and death, trust in the life-giving, grave-conquering King, and you will live with him forever."

Disciples of Jesus know that he is not merely a personal Lord and Savior, worthy of our individual approval. Disciples of Jesus know that he is ultimately the cosmic Lord and Savior, worthy of everyone's eternal praise.

> Confess your need for God in light of Satan's attacks. Ask him to strengthen you with his Word in the power of the Spirit.

OUR FATHER

Blessed be the God and Father of our Lord Jesus Christ,
the Father of mercies and God of all comfort.

2 CORINTHIANS 1:3

THROUGHOUT THE OLD TESTAMENT, God is called by many magnificent names and given numerous majestic titles, but rarely is he described as *Father*—only fifteen times, to be exact. However, when we come to the Gospels, the first four books of the New Testament, we see God described as Father 165 times. All but one of these instances occur when Jesus is specifically teaching his disciples.

For example, in the Sermon on the Mount, when Jesus teaches his disciples to pray, he says, "Pray then like this: 'Our Father in heaven . . .'"[1] This is the first time in all of Scripture where anyone is encouraged to pray to God as Father. The significance is astounding. Followers of Jesus have the distinct privilege of knowing, worshiping, talking to, and relating to God as "our Father."

I am awed when I read 1 John 3:1: "See what kind of love the Father has given to us, that we should be called children of God." John cries, "See it! See the delight the Father has in *you* and *me* as his *children*!"

The rest of the New Testament beckons disciples of Jesus to see that God our Father delights in forgiving us, providing for us, leading us, protecting us, sustaining us, comforting us, directing us, purifying us, disciplining us, giving to us, calling us, and promising us his inheritance. Almighty God experiences pleasure in doing all these things for us as his children.[2] This delight is not designed to be one-sided, though. When Jesus makes us his disciples, he transforms our minds to be like his. As followers of Jesus, we believe his truth and embrace his thoughts without exception. Being a disciple, however, involves much more than mere mental assent to Christ. Being a disciple involves emotional affection for him.

Faith fuels feeling. True intellectual knowledge of God naturally and necessarily involves deep emotional desire for God. If you are a disciple of Jesus, there is a sense of delight that characterizes not only God's attention toward you, but also your affection toward him. Simply put, it is impossible to separate our faith in Jesus from our feelings for him.

Thank God that he has made you his child and given you the privilege of calling him Father. Ask him to give you greater affection for him based on his character and his promises.

DAY 23

BREAD OF LIFE

Man shall not live by bread alone, but by every
word that comes from the mouth of God.

MATTHEW 4:4

WE ALL HAVE NATURAL CRAVINGS—cravings for things such as air, food, water, and companionship. Even the Garden of Eden, the perfect paradise created for Adam and Eve, was not a place where they had no needs or desires. Rather, it was a place where all their needs and desires were met by the God who created them. God told Adam in the Garden of Eden, "You are free to eat and enjoy!"[1]

God has hardwired us with desires for water, food, friends, meaning, and purpose, and each of these cravings is intended to drive us to God as the giver of all good gifts and the sole source of all satisfaction.

With this background in mind, let's look at a time when Jesus spoke to a crowd who was craving more bread. They recounted how Moses had given them bread from heaven, and they asked what kind of bread Jesus could bring to them. Jesus' response was pointed. He said, "It was not Moses who gave you the bread from heaven, but my Father gives you the true bread from heaven."[2] Jesus made it clear that the bread that comes from God is far superior to the manna that came through Moses.

Naturally, the crowds demanded, "Give us this bread always,"[3] and thus the stage was set for a startling declaration from Jesus: "I am the bread of life; whoever comes to me shall not hunger, and whoever believes in me shall never thirst."[4] In one sweeping statement, Jesus communicated to the crowds that he himself was the provision that God had sent to satisfy their souls. In essence, he said, "If you want to be fulfilled, put your faith in me."

This declaration carries huge implications for understanding what it means to live as a disciple of Jesus. To come to Jesus, or to believe in Jesus, is to look to him to satisfy your soul forever. To come to Jesus is to "taste and see that the LORD is good"[5] and to find in him the end of all your desires. To believe in Jesus is to experience an eternal pleasure that far outweighs and outlasts the temporal pleasures of this world.

Acknowledge that Jesus—the Bread of Life—is all you need, and ask God to give you even greater satisfaction in him.

OVERCOMING THE PLEASURES OF SIN

No temptation has overtaken you that is not common to man. God is faithful, and he will not let you be tempted beyond your ability, but with the temptation he will also provide the way of escape, that you may be able to endure it.

1 CORINTHIANS 10:13

SO MANY PROFESSING Christians seem to think that coming to Christ involves letting go of everything they love in the world to embrace things they loathe. They may be willing to "make a decision for Christ" to save their skins for eternity, but truth be told, they really like the ways of this world and really want the things of this world.

So they're caught in the middle. They think they're supposed to try hard to follow Jesus. Yet deep down inside, the pleasures, pursuits, plaudits, and possessions of this world seem far more enticing. Consequently, the lives of these professing Christians are often virtually indistinguishable from the lives of non-Christians. They claim to have faith in Christ, yet they are just as sensual, just as humanistic, and just as materialistic as the world around them.

But this is not the way it's supposed to be. When we truly come to Christ, our thirst is quenched by the fountain of life and our hunger is filled by the bread of heaven. We discover that Jesus is the supreme source of satisfaction, and we want *nothing* apart from him. We realize that he is better than all the pleasures, pursuits, plaudits, and possessions of this world combined. As we trust in Jesus, he transforms our tastes in such a way that we begin to love the things of God that we once hated, and we begin to hate the things of this world that we once loved.

The way to conquer sin is not by working hard to change our deeds, but by trusting Jesus to change our desires. Remember the words of Jesus in John 6:35: "Whoever comes to me shall not hunger, and whoever believes in me shall never thirst."

This is how we overcome the pleasures of sin: by allowing Christ to overcome us with the power of his satisfaction. When lust, lying, greed, or possessions promise pleasure, we fight their appeal with fulfillment in Christ. We know, believe, and trust that Jesus is better, and we refuse to give in to sin because we have found greater gratification in our Savior.

Pray that God would continue to give you a greater desire for him than for the things of this world.

THE PURPOSE OF PRAYER

Pray without ceasing.

1 THESSALONIANS 5:17

MOST PEOPLE THINK about prayer as simply asking for things. "Bless me, help me, protect me, and provide for me"—these are often the only words out of our mouths when we bow our heads. Our prayers are filled with a list of the things we need and the stuff we want. Consequently, in prayer, we're pleased when God responds as we've asked and perplexed when he doesn't.

But God isn't up in heaven with pen and paper waiting for us to pray so he can find out what our needs are. Prayer involves something far deeper—and far more wonderful—than simply informing God of what he already knows.

The purpose of prayer is not for the disciple to bring information to God; the purpose of prayer is for the disciple to experience intimacy with God. That's why Jesus says, "Go into your room and shut the door and pray to your Father who is in secret."[1]

Find a place, Jesus says. Set aside a time. Get alone with God. This one practice will utterly revolutionize your life—not just your prayer life, but your entire life. Something happens that cannot be described in words when we are alone with God. In a quiet place, behind closed doors, when you or I commune with the infinitely great, indescribably good God of the universe, we experience a joy with which nothing else in this world can even begin to compare.

Regardless of the circumstances in our lives, our hearts overflow with thanksgiving, for we know where we deserve to be in our sin and we are confident in where we will one day be because of Christ's sacrifice. In the context of awe-inspiring adoration and affection, heart-breaking confession and contrition, and breath-taking gratitude and praise, we cry out for God to meet our deepest needs. We share the desires of our souls, not because we're trying to give God information, but because we trust in his provision. We commune with God as grateful children who love to be with their Father.

> Thank God for the privilege of prayer. Ask him to give you faith to come to him continually through Christ.

WHAT IS GOD'S WILL FOR MY LIFE?

*For I know the plans I have for you, declares
the LORD, plans for welfare and not for
evil, to give you a future and a hope.*

JEREMIAH 29:11

WHAT IS GOD'S WILL FOR MY LIFE? This is quite possibly the most commonly asked question in Christianity today. We have questions and face decisions all the time, and we find ourselves constantly wondering about God's will in them.

Some decisions are small and seem less significant. *What book should I read this month? Where should we eat today?* Other questions involve large, life-altering decisions. *What career path should I choose? Should I marry? Should we have kids?* And in the middle of it all, we keep coming back to one question: *What does God want me to do?*

We operate as if God's will for us has been lost somewhere. And with all good intentions, we've devised an assortment of methods for finding it.

There's the "Random Finger Method," where we open the Bible at random and put a finger down on a verse to discover God's will for our lives. There's the "Astonishing Miracle Method," where we look for a burning bush like Moses found. The "Striking Coincidence Method" tells us to be on the lookout for unusual coincidences to pop up and tell us what to do.

The list goes on. There's the "Cast the Fleece Method," which requires testing God to see what he wants us to do; the "Still Small Voice Method," which advocates waiting for God to speak to us subtly and quietly; the "Open Door Method," which says that if an opportunity opens up, it is obviously God's will for us to take it; and of course, the "Closed Door Method," which states that if a decision seems difficult, it's obviously *not* God's will for us to make it.

But what if God's will was never intended to be found? In fact, what if it was never hidden from us in the first place? What if searching for God's will misses the entire point of what it means to be a disciple?

Discipleship transforms not only our mind and emotions, but also our will. To quote Paul, "I have been crucified with Christ. It is no longer I who live, but Christ who lives in me."[1] As followers of Jesus, our lives are subsumed in his life, and our ways are totally surrendered to his will.

As such, our aim as disciples of Jesus is not to answer the question, "What is God's will for my life?" It is to walk in God's will on a moment-by-moment, day-by-day basis.

Thank God for revealing himself
in his Word, and ask him
to give you wisdom as you
seek to live for his glory.

WITNESS

You will receive power when the Holy Spirit has come upon you, and you will be my witnesses in Jerusalem and in all Judea and Samaria, and to the end of the earth.

ACTS 1:8

I OFTEN HEAR CHRISTIANS SAY, "Well, I share the gospel when the Holy Spirit leads me." There is some truth here. We want to be led by the Holy Spirit in everything we do. At the same time, we need to remember that the Spirit lives in us for the explicit purpose of spreading the gospel through us. If you have the Holy Spirit in you, you can officially consider yourself led to share the gospel! You don't have to wait for a tingly feeling to go down your spine or a special message to appear from heaven to lead you to tell people about Christ. You just open your mouth and talk about the life, death, and resurrection of Jesus, and you will be carrying out the purpose of Jesus' presence in you. In other words, when you're telling others about the wonder of the gospel, you're carrying out the will of God.

I also hear professing Christians say, "Well, I don't witness with my words; I witness with my life." Again, there's some truth here: We want the character of Christ to be clear in our actions. At the same time, when Jesus told his disciples that they would receive his Spirit and be his witnesses in the world, he wasn't just calling them to be nice to the people around them. Whether in a courtroom or any other circumstance, the basic function of a witness is to speak. Ten of the eleven apostles who heard Jesus' words in Acts 1 were martyred—not because they went into the world doing good deeds, but because they witnessed to the Word of God.

God has given us a gospel to believe, a Spirit to empower, and a language to speak for a purpose—a grand, glorious, global, God-exalting purpose that transcends all of history. For the past two thousand years, God has willed to draw people to himself through the proclamation of his Word by the power of his Spirit, and he simply calls each of us to do the same today. When we are faithful to obey his will, he will show himself faithful to bless his Word.

Ask God to give you the courage and the desire to speak about Christ to your unbelieving family members, friends, and neighbors.

BE THE CHURCH

*Let each of you look not only to his own
interests, but also to the interests of others.*

PHILIPPIANS 2:4

WHAT IS A CHURCH? Most people in America associate the word *church* with a physical building. But when we turn through the pages of the New Testament, we find a very different picture of the church. Instead of a building, we see a body made up of people who share the life of Christ with each other on a day-by-day, week-by-week basis.

This is the pattern that was set by Jesus and his disciples from the beginning. Jesus loved these twelve men, served them, taught them, encouraged them, corrected them, and journeyed through life with them. He spent more time with these twelve disciples than he did with everyone else in his ministry put together. They walked together along lonely roads; they visited together in crowded cities; they sailed and fished together on the Sea of Galilee; they prayed together in the desert and on the mountains; and they worshiped together in the synagogues and at the Temple. During all this time together, Jesus taught them how to live and showed them how to love as he shared his life with them.

In the same way, the New Testament envisions followers of Jesus living alongside one another for the sake of one another. The Bible portrays the church as a community of

Christians who care for one another, love one another, host one another, receive one another, honor one another, serve one another, instruct one another, forgive one another, motivate one another, build up one another, encourage one another, comfort one another, pray for one another, confess sin to one another, esteem one another, edify one another, teach one another, show kindness to one another, give to one another, rejoice with one another, weep with one another, hurt with one another, and restore one another.[1]

All these "one anothers" combine to paint a picture of people who don't just come to a building filled with customized programs, but who have decided to lay down their lives to love one another. Simply put, the church is a community of Christians who love one another and long for each other to know and grow in Christ.

> Pray for the spiritual health of your church. Ask God to shape it by his Word and to use it for the spread of his gospel.

REBUKE AND REFLECT

Two are better than one, because they have a good reward for their toil. For if they fall, one will lift up his fellow. But woe to him who is alone when he falls and has not another to lift him up!

ECCLESIASTES 4:9-10

WE LIVE IN a day when it's easy, popular, and even preferred for people to sit back and say, "Well, what other people do is between them and God. Their sin is their life, their decision, and their responsibility."

But aren't you glad this isn't how God responds to us? Aren't you glad he pursues us despite our sin and pulls us away from that which would destroy us? And don't we want people in our lives who will love us enough to look out for us when we begin to walk down a road of sinful destruction?

Dietrich Bonhoeffer once said, "Nothing can be more cruel than the tenderness that consigns another to his sin. Nothing can be more compassionate than the severe rebuke that calls a brother back from the path of sin."[1]

God is a gracious Father who seeks after his wandering children, and we reflect his grace when we care for brothers and sisters who are caught in sin. Obviously, God alone has ultimate authority to judge. Yet, in Matthew 7:5, Jesus tells his disciples to remove sin in their own lives and then help others remove sin from their lives. The last thing we need to do when a brother or sister is continually walking into sin is to say, "Well, it's not my place to judge."

Being a member of a church means so much

more than standing next to someone and singing songs together once a week. Being a member of a church means realizing that we are responsible for helping our brothers and sisters in Christ to grow as disciples of Jesus. In the same way, they are responsible for helping us.

We desperately need each other in the daily fight to follow Jesus in a world that's full of sin. For as Christians lock their arms and lives together with one another in local churches, nothing has the power to stop the global spread of God's gospel to the ends of the earth.

Thank God for the gift of brothers and sisters in Christ in the church. Ask him to give you a willingness to receive rebukes when necessary.

MAKING DISCIPLES

Let your light shine before others, so that they may see your good works and give glory to your Father who is in heaven.

MATTHEW 5:16

DISCIPLE-MAKING INVOLVES FAR more than merely leading people to trust in Jesus; disciple-making involves teaching people to *follow* Jesus. This means we must *show* people what the life of Christ looks like in action.

The active nature of the Christian life is clearly portrayed in what Paul wrote to the new brothers and sisters in Thessalonica:

> Our gospel came to you not only in word, but also in power and in the Holy Spirit and with full conviction. You know what kind of men we proved to be among you for your sake. And you became imitators of us and of the Lord, for you received the word in much affliction, with the joy of the Holy Spirit.[1]

Paul, Silas, and Timothy had spoken about the power of the gospel with their lips while they showed the effects of the gospel in their lives. They had been intentional about leading lives worthy of imitation, in order to share the gospel with the men and women of Thessalonica. And when the Thessalonians came to faith in Christ, they began to follow the example that had been set by these three brothers.

This is part of what it means for us as disciples to make disciples. In our homes and our workplaces; in our families and with our friends; as husbands, wives, moms, dads, sons, daughters, employers, employees, teachers, coaches, lawyers, doctors, janitors, consultants, waiters, salespeople, and accountants, you and I are to intentionally lead lives that are worthy of imitation. Through modeling the character of Christ, speaking the truth of Christ, and showing the love of Christ, we commend the gospel of Christ to people all around us every day. In the process, we teach people to obey all that Christ has commanded us.

In the great commission, Jesus tells all his disciples to go, baptize, and teach people to obey everything he has commanded them. This kind of teaching doesn't require a special gifting or a specific setting. This kind of teaching happens all over the place—in homes, neighborhoods, workplaces, on car rides, in meetings, and over meals—in the context of where we live, work, and play every day.

This is the picture of Christ's church that we see in Scripture: a community of faith saturating their conversations with the Word of God wherever they go—in their homes, where they work, and wherever else they walk.

Pray that disciples would be made in your own community and across the globe. Ask the Lord to send workers to those places where there is little or no access to the gospel.

PROCLAIM THE GOSPEL

The harvest is plentiful, but the laborers are few; therefore pray earnestly to the Lord of the harvest to send out laborers into his harvest.

MATTHEW 9:37-38

I GIVE YOU a portrait of the church at its inception.

A small band of men responded to a life-changing invitation: "Follow me, and I will make you fishers of men."[1] Over the next three years, they watched Jesus, listened to him, and learned from him how to love, teach, and serve others the same way that he did.

Then came the moment when they saw him die on a cross for their sins, only to rise from the dead three days later. Soon thereafter, he gathered them on a mountainside and said to them, "All authority in heaven and on earth has been given to me. Go therefore and make disciples of all nations, baptizing them in the name of the Father and of the Son and of the Holy Spirit, teaching them to observe all that I have commanded you. And behold, I am with you always, to the end of the age."[2]

True to his promise, Jesus sent his Spirit to his disciples, and immediately they began proclaiming the gospel. In the days that followed, they scattered from Jerusalem to Judea to Samaria to the ends of the earth, and within one generation, their numbers grew to more than four hundred times what they were when they started.

Did they succeed because they had extravagant buildings and entertaining programs? No.

The spread of the gospel took place primarily because ordinary people empowered by an extraordinary presence proclaimed the gospel everywhere they went. It was anonymous Christians (that is, not the original disciples) who first took the gospel to Judea and Samaria, and it was unnamed believers who founded the church at Antioch, which became a base for mission to the Gentile world. The Good News of Jesus spread through everyday people going from house to house, leading people to faith.

This is how the gospel penetrated the world during the first century: disciples making disciples. Christians were not known for association with Christ and his church; instead, they were known for complete abandonment to Christ and his cause. The great commission was not a choice for them to consider, but a command for them to obey. And though they faced untold trials and unthinkable persecution, they experienced unimaginable joy as they joined with Jesus in the advancement of his Kingdom.

> Ask God to help you and your church leaders rely on his wisdom and power working through the church.

SPEAK

In your hearts honor Christ the Lord as holy, always being prepared to make a defense to anyone who asks you for a reason for the hope that is in you.

1 PETER 3:15

CONSIDER THE GOSPEL: the Good News that the just and gracious God of the universe has looked upon hopelessly sinful people and sent his Son, Jesus Christ—God in the flesh—to bear his wrath against sin on the cross and to show his power over sin in the Resurrection so that everyone who turns from sin and trusts in him will be reconciled to God forever.

In this gospel, we find various facets or components that we all can articulate. Every follower of Christ knows who God is, what man's ultimate problem is, who Jesus is and what he has done, how someone can be saved, and how important it is for people to be saved. So, let's incorporate the character of God, the sinfulness of man, the sufficiency of Christ, the necessity of faith, and the urgency of eternity into our everyday conversations.

Let's speak continually to the people around us about God as someone we know, love, and worship. Let's put God's character on display every day before people who may not yet believe in him. Let's speak about God as Creator, as Judge, and as Savior in the context of our everyday conversations.

Let's speak about the ultimate problem of humanity: *sin*. Let's speak humbly about the seriousness of sin in our lives and in a world full of evil, suffering, sickness, pain, and death.

Let's talk about Jesus' life—the people he healed, things he taught, miracles he performed, and ways he served. Let's speak about his death. And let's proclaim his resurrection.

What could we do in our lives that would be more valuable than this? What else might we do today that would be more significant than telling others that the God of the universe loves them and desires for them to know him and be saved from their sins forever? And what could be more exhilarating than seeing a person's life altered for all of eternity right before our eyes as he or she turns from sin and trusts in Christ as Savior?

For the next ten billion years and beyond, that person's life—and the lives of scores of other people he or she encounters in the future—will be completely different because of what you or I have the opportunity to say today.

> Pray that God would use you
> to bear witness to the gospel
> in the midst of your daily
> interactions with unbelievers.

MAKE DISCIPLES IN ALL NATIONS

How then will they call on him in whom they have not believed? And how are they to believe in him of whom they have never heard? And how are they to hear without someone preaching?

ROMANS 10:14

AS DISCIPLES OF JESUS, we share, show, and teach God's Word. This is what it means to make disciples, and Jesus told us to do this in all nations. The phrase that Jesus uses for "all nations" in Matthew 28:19 is *panta ta ethne*, which literally means all the ethnicities, or peoples, of the world.

Many people misunderstand this verse, thinking that Jesus is talking about nations like we think of nations today. Approximately two hundred geopolitical nations exist today, but these are not the nations that Jesus is referring to. He was talking about families, tribes, and clans that are now commonly called people groups. Biblical, anthropological, and missiological scholars have looked at the ethnicities represented around the world and have identified more than eleven thousand different people groups composed of people who share similar cultural and linguistic characteristics.

Interestingly, the Bible ends with a portrait of men and women from every single one of these people groups represented around the throne of Christ, singing the praises of God. The book of Revelation envisions a scene with "a great multitude that no one could number, from every nation, from all tribes and peoples and languages, standing before the throne and before the Lamb."[1]

Clearly, God's eternal purpose is to save people, through Christ, from every people group in the world. So naturally Jesus commands his disciples to go and make disciples worldwide. This is a specific command for you and me as disciples of Jesus to make disciples of Jesus among every people group on the planet.

More than six thousand people groups comprising nearly two billion people in the world are classified as unreached, meaning they will likely be born, live, and die without ever hearing about how they can be saved from their sins through Christ.

This is not acceptable for disciples of Jesus. Our Savior has given us a command to make disciples of every people group, and we have no option but to obey. Nor would we want to take any other option. We who have the life of Christ yearn to spread the love of Christ.

Ask God to use your church to reach unreached people groups through sending workers, through long-term partnerships with missionaries, and through sacrificial giving.

LIVING CHURCH

I heard the voice of the Lord saying, "Whom
shall I send, and who will go for us?"
Then I said, "Here I am! Send me."

ISAIAH 6:8

IMAGINE YOUR CHURCH. If you had nothing but people—no buildings, no programs, no staff, and no activities—and you were charged with spreading the gospel to the whole world, where would you begin? Would you start by spending millions of dollars on a building to meet in? Not if you really believed God's Word. The Bible never tells us to construct a "house of worship." Instead, the Bible says that we as God's people *are* the house of worship. The New Testament never tells us to build a place for people to come to us; instead, it commands us to invest our lives *going* to people.

Similarly, if we really believed the Bible, we probably wouldn't limit ministry to a team of ministers who lead the church. Instead, we would all go. Every single one of us. We would scatter as rapidly as possible to make the gospel known to as many people as possible as quickly as possible.

It would be difficult, though, and probably costly. So even as we scattered, we would gather together periodically. The purpose of our gathering would not be to sit in a class, it would be to share our lives—to share the hurts and joys we are experiencing as we spend our lives spreading the gospel to the ends of the earth. We would encourage one another, teach one another, worship with one another, give to one another, and then we would scatter again to make the gospel of Jesus known to more people. We would do this week after week and year after year, and we would not stop until the Good News of Jesus spread from our houses to our communities to our cities to the nations.

Real disciples want to be part of a movement like that. They want to be part of a people who have forsaken every earthly ambition in favor of one eternal aspiration: to see disciples made and churches multiplied.

This kind of movement involves all of us. Ordinary people spreading the gospel in extraordinary ways all over the world. Men and women from diverse backgrounds with different gifts and distinct platforms making disciples and multiplying churches through every domain of society in every place on the planet. This is God's design for his church, and disciples of Jesus must not settle for anything less.

> Confess your dependence
> on God. Ask him to use
> you and your church for the
> accomplishment of his purposes.

A CALL WORTH DYING FOR

By this we know love, that he laid down his life for us,
and we ought to lay down our lives for the brothers.

1 JOHN 3:16

TWO THOUSAND YEARS AGO, Jesus wandered the streets and byways of Israel. He was initiating a revolution, but his revolution didn't revolve around the masses or multitudes. It revolved around a few men. Those few disciples would learn to think like Jesus, love like Jesus, teach like Jesus, live like Jesus, and serve like Jesus. As Jesus transformed his followers, they became fishers of men, and we have the gospel today because they were faithful in making more disciple-makers.

So, let us be faithful to do the same. We are followers of Jesus. We have died to ourselves, and we now live in Christ. He has saved us from our sins and has satisfied our souls. He has transformed our minds with his truth, fulfilled our desires with his joy, and conformed our ways to his will. He has joined us together in bodies of believers called local churches for the accomplishment of one all-consuming commission: the declaration of his gospel and the display of his glory to all the peoples of the world.

This task involves all of us. No child of God is intended by God to be sidelined as a spectator in the great commission. Every child of God has been invited by God to be on the front lines of history's supreme mission. Every disciple of Jesus has been called, loved, created, and saved to make disciples of Jesus who make disciples of Jesus who make disciples of Jesus until the grace of God is enjoyed and the glory of God is exalted among every people group on the planet. And on that day, every disciple of Jesus—every true and authentic follower of Christ and fisher of men—will see the Savior's face and behold the Father's splendor in a scene of indescribable beauty and everlasting bliss that will never, ever fade away.

This is a call worth dying for.

This is a King worth living for.

Pray that God, by his grace, would sustain your faith and, regardless of the cost, give you a greater desire to follow Christ.

NOTES

INTRODUCTION
1. Dawson Trotman, "Born to Reproduce," 5, 12. Retrieved from Discipleship Library, http://www.discipleshiplibrary .com/pdfs/AA094.pdf.
2. Matthew 4:19

DAY 1: FOLLOW ME
1. Matthew 4:19.
2. See Matthew 16:24; Mark 8:34; Luke 9:23.

DAY 2: THE GATE IS NARROW
1. Matthew 7:13-14

DAY 3: GIVE UP EVERYTHING
1. Oswald Chambers, *My Utmost for His Highest*, entry for May 30, https://utmost.org/yes%E2%80%94-but.
2. Luke 14:26-27, 33
3. Chambers, *My Utmost*, May 30.

DAY 4: BELIEVE AND CONFESS
1. John 3:16
2. Acts 16:31
3. Romans 10:9
4. See James 2:19.

DAY 5: REPENT AND CHANGE
1. See Matthew 4:17.
2. Galatians 2:20

DAY 7: LOOK AT THE CROSS
1. John 3:36, NIV
2. Isaiah 53:5-6, italics added.

DAY 8: ONE LOST SHEEP
1. Ephesians 1:3-6
2. Luke 15:4-7

DAY 10: COME TO ME
1. This invitation occurs more than a dozen times in the Gospels, including Matthew 4:19, Mark 2:14, Luke 9:59, and John 1:43, italics added.
2. John 14:6, italics added.

DAY 11: NEVER ENOUGH
1. John 3:5
2. Ezekiel 36:25-27

DAY 13: THE GOOD NEWS OF CHRIST
1. Matthew 9:2

DAY 14: THE ESSENCE OF THE CHRISTIAN LIFE
1. Ezekiel 36:26-27
2. Galatians 2:20, author's paraphrase.
3. Romans 8:10-11

DAY 15: FISHERS OF MEN
1. Matthew 4:19
2. Matthew 28:19-20

DAY 16: SUPERNATURALLY COMPELLED
1. Matthew 4:19

DAY 17: LORD AND SAVIOR
1. Philippians 2:10-11

DAY 18: THE SPIRIT OF TRUTH
1. Barna Group, "Most American Christians Do Not Believe that Satan or the Holy Spirit Exist," *Research Releases in*

Faith & Christianity, April 13, 2009; www.barna.com/
research/most-american-christians-do-not-believe-that-
satan-or-the-holy-spirit-exist.
2. John 14:17, 26
3. John 8:31-32; 15:7

DAY 19: THE REALITY OF THE RESURRECTION
1. See 1 Corinthians 15:12-19.

DAY 20: HEAVEN AND HELL
1. See Luke 16:22-23 and Matthew 22:13.
2. See 2 Thessalonians 1:9.
3. John 11:25-26
4. John 3:16
5. See John 14:1-6.
6. Revelation 21:1, 4
7. Matthew 4:19

DAY 21: SPIRITUAL BATTLE
1. See Galatians 2:20.
2. Luke 24:47
3. Ephesians 1:20-21

DAY 22: OUR FATHER
1. Matthew 6:9
2. See Matthew 6:11-15 (forgiving); Matthew 6:25-33
   (providing); Romans 8:14 (leading); Romans 8:15
   (protecting); 1 Corinthians 8:6 (sustaining); 2 Corinthians
   1:3 (comforting); 1 Thessalonians 3:11 (directing);
   1 Thessalonians 3:13 (purifying); Hebrews 12:5-11
   (disciplining); James 1:17 (giving to); Jude 1:1 (calling);
   Colossians 1:12 (promising his inheritance).

DAY 23: BREAD OF LIFE
1. See Genesis 2:16.
2. John 6:32
3. John 6:34
4. John 6:35
5. Psalm 34:8

DAY 25: THE PURPOSE OF PRAYER
1. Matthew 6:6

DAY 26: WHAT IS GOD'S WILL FOR MY LIFE?
1. Galatians 2:20

DAY 28: BE THE CHURCH
1. See 1 Corinthians 12:25 (caring); John 13:34-35 (loving); 1 Peter 4:9 (hosting); Romans 15:7 (receiving); Romans 12:10 (honoring); Galatians 5:13 (serving); Romans 15:14 (instructing); Colossians 3:13 (forgiving); Hebrews 10:24 (motivating); 1 Thessalonians 5:13 (building up); 1 Thessalonians 5:11 (encouraging); 2 Corinthians 1:3-7 (comforting); James 5:16 (praying for and confessing sin to); Philippians 2:3 (esteeming); Romans 14:19 (edifying); Colossians 3:16 (teaching); Ephesians 4:32 (showing kindness to); Acts 2:45 and 2 Corinthians 8–9 (giving to); Romans 12:15 (weeping with); 1 Corinthians 12:27 (rejoicing with); Galatians 6:1-5 and Matthew 18:15-20 (restoring).

DAY 29: REBUKE AND REFLECT
1. Dietrich Bonhoeffer, *Life Together* (New York: Harper & Row, 1954), 107.

DAY 30: MAKING DISCIPLES
1. 1 Thessalonians 1:5-6

DAY 31: PROCLAIM THE GOSPEL
1. Matthew 4:19
2. Matthew 28:18-20

DAY 33: MAKE DISCIPLES IN ALL NATIONS
1. Revelation 7:9

ABOUT THE AUTHOR

DAVID PLATT IS THE AUTHOR of three *New York Times* bestsellers, including *Follow Me* and *Radical*. He is lead pastor at McLean Bible Church in metro Washington, DC; former president of the International Mission Board; and founder of Radical, Inc., a resource ministry that serves churches in accomplishing the global mission of Christ. Platt received his master of divinity, master of theology, and doctor of philosophy from New Orleans Baptist Theological Seminary. He lives in Virginia with his wife and four children.

ARE YOU READY TO BECOME A FOLLOWER OF CHRIST?

The call to follow Jesus is not simply an invitation to pray a prayer; it is a summons to lose your life . . . and to find new life in him. In *Follow Me*, David Platt reveals a biblical picture of what it truly means to be a Christian.

ARE *YOU* READY TO
COUNTER
CULTURE?

Everywhere we turn, battle lines are being drawn. Seemingly overnight, culture has shifted to the point where right and wrong are no longer measured by universal truth but by popular opinion.

In *Counter Culture*, David Platt shows Christians how to actively take a stand on such issues as poverty, sex trafficking, marriage, abortion, racism, and religious liberty, and challenges us to become passionate, unwavering voices for Christ.

Additional study materials are available online and in a bookstore near you. To learn more about how you can counter culture, please visit us at www.counterculturebook.com.

CP0851